To my Tank man
who encouraged me to write again,
my family, friends, my comrades and to all Filipinos
across the globe without whom this book would have
been completed ages ago.

YOU'RE ALL I WANT

Past, I want to bring back the past,
The time when we were still sweet,
Always I think every night,
Happiness on us can't get lost,
Tears in my eyes can't really hide it,
Because you're always in my sight.

You mend my broken heart,
But easily you broke.
You healed my pain,
But easily you hurt me.
You caress me,
But easily you changed.
How can I forget the past?

Your thoughtfulness, whom I can search for?
Your carefulness, can I just forget it?
Definitely I can't...
Because you're all I want.

TO MY INSPIRATION

I wonder how it whips the zephyrs that flee,

In a churlish yet blissful den,

Throttling though the gushing of glee,

And seized a million mirth now and then?

I wonder how the flowers bloom,

In a pristine moment of single day,

Glaring it's beauty to the groom,

Whom does she like all the way?

I wonder how a tyke titillating,

In a shallow way of enjoyment,

As nobody could cling,

Even for just a moment?

And how I wonder to a damsel in distress,

Who trapped into peril,

But a knight in shinin' armour caress,

Rescuing decisively with a thrill?

I feel the zippy breeze of cold December,

Creeping up thru my veins the sensation,

Why thee to remember,

Yuletide season with applause fascination?

Aristocrat, oh my chivalry!

Amending my appetite of love,

Trampled my primitive sanctuary,

And animate me like a dove?

My glistening eyes on you,

Gnawing the fear deep within,

My coy heart sough,

You're my inspiration in this domain.

Amid the abyss that divides us,

With your finicky type,

And vile manner that's quite a fuss,

I grope but love without gyp.

As a sophomore student I'm old enough,

To spill out one word as I vow,

You build me authentically tough,

Tossing the allurements that sow.

Murmur of my voice you listen!

Come to my dale words of word,

In my studies you are my inspiration,

The Romeo that dispenses my world.

SEDUCTION

Allurements...allurements...allurements...

Please don't enthral my feelings,

I am so fragile when it comes to these cases,

You can easily captivate me without any assaults.

Yes, you seduce me wholly...

I tried to elude but it's too late,

Your irresistible kisses touching my lips so great,

And enslave me like your lady totally.

You hinder me every step of my way...

The more I ignore that uncertainty creeping up on my body,

The more you insist and pat your kiss passionately,

And there you drive me so crazy.

Somewhere in my mind trying to obviate that trap...

But I was so tipsy every move you clasp,

Can't no longer clash your intense deed I want to dump,

Because all of the sudden we're both on the top.

All I know, nobody can portray how completely woman I am...

For once in my life I feel like a precious gem,

And surely I'll treasure deep within,

Because I love you...beloved of mine.

FRAUDULENCE

You came into my life as if a choice,
Knowing it's about time to rejoice,
You topple my heart as I hear your voice,
No bother at all with my nonsense noise.

The darkened trail of my life now flashing,
The never ending corridor now ceasing,
Wounded heart of mine seems mending,
And grief music turned out romantically flowing.

Now my life suddenly there's a plan,
Just like Lois Lane kissing Superman,
All I can feel is marvellous in this domain,
When you're near I just can't explain.

But why do I let myself live with that trickery?
You evoke my fragileness like a mystery,
The enticement you showed can't resist really
I know, time to bound it ends, for being silly.

I should stop on pretending now to assure,

Goodbye...though it's painful I'll endure,

Bear on your mind that I love you endlessly

Because my heart will always beat restlessly.

My Sweet Obsession

Amid the crowd, your devilish gorgeous face mesmerise me,

Those enchanting eyes when you gaze captivated me,

Your nose that stand firm cheer my very heart,

Voluptuous lips that bears like a minx alluring my whole being,

Oh, that aristocrat yet charismatic face tugging my heart.

You were as though a knight in shinin' armour,

Claiming my heart beyond the agony of life like a warrior.

Whenever you're near I feel like a taciturn mistress,

Tranquillity remained and my senses turned into distress...

I am, but beyond your utmost control and visionary den.

You actually dispense my innocence by your caress,

As you intimately touch every inch of my body--heavenly!

Your expertise lips exhaust my mind, such incomparable kisses

No man in this world enslave me like this but you my sweety

My sweet obsession be with me, now, tomorrow and 'till eternity!

Don't Make me Fall In Love Again

As I ceased walking in the middle of wilderness,

I realise, I need to find the way-out from the darkness,

Truly I need to evade the cliff of sadness,

Yet there you are..looking sharp in madness.

Sorrow that lingering in my heart vanished totally.

You just let that music play constantly....

Dancing in fancy dress like a legendary...

You let me feel the serenity of real sanctuary.

Honestly, you lighten up the darkened trail of my life,

You held my hands when I'm about to fall,

You actually pour out the blissfulness that once left me behind,

And you painted the rainbow in the sky.

All the while, I need to be cautious to this feelings that I'm wearing,

Because I was marooned to your powerful stares you're carrying,

And yes, you make me feel uneasy whenever you're around,

But pleading before you, don't make me fall for you.

The Past

Sometimes it's hard to let go,
Days gone by that lucidly glow,
Way back then let them know,
Bursting emotions are about to blow!

They say leave behind the past,
Memoirs must need to cast,
Treasure them but opt to blast,
Then walk away and run so fast.

Easy for you to say and judge,
Knowing it's just a mere smudge,
Surpass my race then give me a nudge,
If the olden days shouldn't drudge.

I tell you I'm not being ludicrous,
Nor acting like unscrupulous,
Do not think I am ridiculous,
Gracious past is voluminous.

My Polynomial Love

The equation of my love is incomparable,
No algebraic expression is imponderable,
When I see your smile that is admirable,
Neither subtraction or division is intolerable,
As the exponent of my heart is unconquerable.

No one can intercept my feelings towards you,
Nor substitute my fervour everytime I see you,
Through addition and multiplication yes it's true,
My love for you will function and always grew,
Graphing my genuine affection is just a whew!

Believe it or not it's like a linear function,
Straight from my heart you give a sanction,
You shape me like a parabola in action,
Like a cubic formula as my presumption,
The perimeter of my soul has no destruction.

As a senior high I am capable and not just a bluff,
To justify the coefficient of my senses and engulf,
You are the key of all the aridity, now I can puff,
You and me will merge as one please don't rebuff,
From left to right and negative to positive stuff.

My fascination will never just end,
No distinction points can determine nor send,
You are my x-axis as my studies tend,
But will never be an ex like others trend,
'Cause you are the symmetrical godsend.

Like I said, my numerical feelings is sublime,
That no one can solve like a number prime,
Nor measure or sketch like a paradigm,
The solution is clear, you'll get it sometime,
You and I will easily graph for a lifetime.

Police Officer's Vow

The moment I laid my eyes on you,
You became my target out of the blue,
You trigger my feelings and I don't have a clue,
My heart beats faster than an ammo to get through,
Bulls eye! You're like a top gun to break into.

Yes, you're now the prime suspect of my case,
You murder my heart by your bewitching face,
Like a fugitive I'm hunting you and trace,
To state the Miranda Doctrine of my soul and lace,
No need for evidence nor confidentiality to take place.

Straight to your heart you detained me though,
With no bail or appeal to file and bestow,
And I swear this is not a compliance to throw,
Either you investigate me my testimony will show,
Because I love you from Reclusion Perpetua to death row!

YOUR IDEAL MAN IS NOT YOUR MAN

We often mention the qualities of our ideal man,

We've been very vocal about our feelings as if we can...

Find the man we're looking for just like our plan,

Proudly show to the whole world their kind of clan.

He must be good looking, sharp, and hot like a hero,

Ideally kind, honest and gentleman to follow,

Must have a sense of humour and stable to show,

Most of all, he must be a one-woman-man and not a weirdo.

Now look at your man, you realise you tick only 2 on your list,

You marry a man that few qualities he carries on your checklist,

Then you came asking yourself, does an ideal man do exist?

Or, you're just egotistically naïve in this world full of twists?

Looking for ideal man is like watching a fantasy,

It is not though a fictional story but a total reality,

That needs to relinquish within your insanity,

Because your ideal man is not your man, actually.

Move On...

They said patience is virtue,

That, choose heart over mind,

That, live..love..and fight as you continue,

Life is too short to just leave behind.

But how long would you be able to endure?

Aren't you acting immature?

Why don't you try to be closer to nature?

Don't you think you're just totally allured?

It is not destiny that dictates our fate,

Nor a fairy tale story with a happy ending,

Let it be accepted 'coz it's not yet too late,

Just open your eyes and stop pretending.

Remember that life is like a holographic,

Sometimes you were enthralled like a magic,

Embracing the joy and feeling fantastic,

But in the end you will be problematic.

So, better yet move on and be content,

Start your life and learn the concept,

Love is when two people are correspondent,

No secrets nor turned you into despondent.

GOODBYE...

All these days I never dare quitted,

From endurance to sacrifices I didn't demanded,

With a veil of tears that drowned me,

Pain and griefings slowly killing me,

Still... my faith in you domineer my being,

Because I love you and I'm not just dreaming.

My heart blinded me as everybody dwells,

I became as though a deaf before their very eyes,

But deep inside me desperation canopied me,

Kneeling before God, I need to be free,

Goodbye is the hardest word to utter,

Pointless affection has to end 'cos you're not my lover.

Goodbye...you're not worthy as my man...

My Other Half

Like a mission you came tactically like an elite force,
You neutralised my insensitive heart in such a course,
Unmasking your good intentions as a source,
Winning my heart and mind indeed you enforce.

God is such an enigmatic in scribing our story,
It was truly written in the stars and not in fury,
Scots-Pinay would be our badge to carry,
That no one can reform a dullness from merry.

No amount of depths can deter if your intention is pure,
Or either a disaster can intimidate you if your love is true,
Cultures differences wouldn't be an obstruction for sure,
Because true love conquers all and torment is about to cure.

Combating our divergence before is quite an inferno,
Our consciousness to react is as faster like an ammo,
You're the lead scout and I'm the navigator like Commando,
As I opened my eyes I realised you're my other half as I know.

HIGHSCHOOL LIFE

Highschool is the beginning of growth,
It is where you can see your worth,
Puberty starts and life will be rolling in this earth,
Attitudes and emotions will change both.

Highschool life is the happiest moment,
You'll meet your peers in such a concept,
Creating camaraderie is everybody's involvement,
Where you can hear a sweet and sour comment.

Be careful to choose your group of friends,
If you got a bad omen better yet ends,
Be wise and vigilant to give trust and extends,
Some pals are fake and they just pretend.

Once you met that long awaiting friendship,
Build a strong and exceptional relationship,
A bond that is unbreakable like a kinship,
That no matter what, you can conquer hardship.

Enjoy every single day of your Highschool life,
Focus onto the happiness and not in armed strife,
Let music play and chuckles be heard like a fife,

Let love prevail and togetherness will be rife.

In laughter and in tears you will be together,

Sustain the good rapport you have like a brother,

At the end of the day you will go further,

But your friendship will remain forever!

TO MY GRANNY IN HEAVEN

It's been a decade since you've gone,
But all your advices will remain undone,
Just like a guidebook in school for everyone,
It will be continued and spread to anyone.

You often remind us to be silent,
Whenever somebody's verbally violent,
Nor belittling us...you just tell not to be insurgent,
Leave it to God and simply keep quiet.
I vividly remember how pure your heart Granny,
Your good peculiarities is quite uncanny,
I never seen you like a loser or feeling crummy,
Hence, you're always optimistic and happy.

All your anecdotes and non-fiction kept within my head,
From World War II to beyond imagination stories to be said,
You served our country even in simplest way,
Veterans to be called that needed to say.

Goosebumps creeping up on me whenever I disclosed,
When you're fighting death as they imposed,
At 3 AM you can hear the resounding bell that's so close...
Into your ears that breaks the silence of the night as it goes.

Every details of your stories is utterly amazing,
When you reached the stairs of heaven in such a praising,
And meet St. Peter browsing his massive book and saying...

"Your name wasn't here yet" and so you're suddenly arising!
Your second life brings 7 decades to count,
Now here's your granddaughter to recount,
Proudly honouring you as best Granny in the world,
Your good deeds will never just be hurled.

All praises to your kindness my dearest Granny!

MY VALENTINE

Two broken hearts find its own way in this domain,

From the other side of the world, you navigate the terrain.

You trampled as though a brave heart just to attain,

The missing part of your story now you obtain,

Yes, the next chapter of our episode is about to explain.

How genius Cupid could be?

To aim his magical arrow and flee,

From the frosty land to roasting sea,

Landed to the strictly guarded camp as I see,

Straight to my busted heart, sadness turned into glee.

Now that it's Valentine I want you to know,

How thankful I am to be your soulmate and I'll show,

You and I stand still no matter what... Yes, I owe!

Tough days ended and now we're grateful, though

Stick together like a last man army in the battle row.

WILL YOU BE MY VALENTINE?

How whimsical teenage await for Valentine,

Considering as though a significant story line

For the whole year that intertwine,

Life that riddles feeling like sparkling wine.

A view of the future that can be sublime.

Now I tell you here's my rendition,

Painting your sky with constant transition,

No matter how unimaginable I will petition,

The Day is coming and I need your decision,

Will you be my dazzling Valentine?

Mother's Day Special

Today is the celebration of Mother's Day,
Nanang (Mum) You might be miles away,
You never forget to remind me and relay,
To take care of myself and always pray.

How I wish I could bring you here,
Have a chat next to me as I hear,
Your advices and wisdom close to my ear,
'Coz I feel at ease and no fear.

We're the proudest to have you as our Mother,
For raising us well and not to suffer,
You taught us how to be tougher,
And filled our hearts with love and not to wonder.

We may not be vocal in saying I love you,
But our action speaks louder as we do,
Seeing you happy and not being blue...
Is our desire as your children, yes, it's true!

AYE SCOTLAND

Aye! Scotland sublime sanctuary,
From the loch view that is extraordinary...
To pristine hillock and ben that is legendary,
That mesmerises even the fairy.

Thistle and daffodil flowers on spring,
Snowdrop, why so stunning?
Look at the golden yellow trees that bring,
Autumn season, why so dazzling?

Those gigantic castles that stand,
From 11th century of command,
Ancient fortress and timberland,
Isn't it astonishing to understand?

Hiking trails or wee walk is everywhere,
Into the woods nor reservoir quite debonair,
Hamlet yet splendid to live and bare,
Bonnie and placidity you can't compare.

Scots men are cordial and cheeky,
Tough, warrior and not a freaky,
Do not terrorise them and you'll be squeaky,
See Brave Heart?... He's undeniably gritty!

MOTHER EARTH

Look at the golden-yellow trees around,
Leaves that starts falling onto the ground,
Yet the beauty perfectly unveil surround,
That bewitches our eyes and astound.

Feel the autumn breeze that brings,
Robins, crows and chaffinch that sings,
Birds slowly dwindle on the strings,
As winter approaches, that stiffs their wings.

Like a captivating sunset in briny ocean,
With vibrant horizon that gives its emotion,
As twilight embrace the harmonic wavy motion,
That brings accord and joy of locomotion.

See the grey sky manifest before your eyes,
Slowly decaying the allurements of the sunrise,
Maple leaves change like a chameleon in disguise,
And Mother earth... She cuts off her ties...

LEGENDARY MOUNTAIN

Nature is God's architectonic design,
Like mountain so high and enshrine,
Its beauty is mesmerising and divine,
That no one can decimate the lifeline.

As you climb into the edge part,
So stiff that drained you at the start,
But when touching the top heart,
Feeling glorious to perceive the art.

The overlooking sight that enchant,
That makes your heart sing and chant,
With clouds so near that supplant,
The scepticism to mount or grant.

But volcanic eruption is chaotic,
When raging it's like a demonic,
Earthquake prompt the electric,
That destroys the view of its exotic.

Natural disaster is God's actions,
That no one can halt its violations,
So mind to enjoy the attractions,

And embrace with all satisfactions.

ONLY FEW CAN UNDERSTAND...

PTSD…an invisible illness that people may not know,

An illness that anytime the victim could blow,

But nobody cares and compassion hasn't show,

Because only a few can understand….

Others discerned as if a contagious disease,

They try to mock the poor victims and they tease,

Cracking up is not an excuse for them to please,

Because only a few can understand…

Who can tell that a person with PTSD is a monster?

Isn't it too harsh for you to judge them and better yet foster?

Why not listen to their sentiments to make them stronger?

…That's because only a few can understand…

You have no idea the agony and hell they've been through,

That in their entire life they're fighting demons to drew,

Their angers killing them, but people never knew,

Because only a few can understand…

You are not upright nor perfect for them to degrade,

Hence, you should help them and not to evade,

You shouldn't bully them like nobody or played,

Because....only few can understand...

Redemption

At young age, hyperactive is normally evolve,

Playing freely without limitation involve,

No guidance at all whether it is approve,

To do things which I know no need to resolve.

As times passing by, my world turned into hell,

Manic feelings can't control and I want to yell,

I turn around to seek help 'coz I'm under spell,

But nobody held a hand and gave me a shell.

How devastating my world could be?

Why are archons trying to control me?

But I toughly face 'coz I clearly see,

A soulmate that leads me to thee.

Yes, you are my mate as I linger in this terrain,

My best friend in laughter and in tears through the rain,

My buddy in every move we take in this domain...

My dear wife, you're the only one who listened when I explained!

COMMANDO MESMERIZE

Way back then, she is but a wee-timid lassie in their place,
Always been hiding like a squirrel as if they have to chase,
Too shy to show up for no reason and so she glace,
Her flaws conquering her being that bring her in the space,
Feeling like a loser and she didn't even bother to mace.

She has no phobia nor disability,
But scared of the dark like insanity,
Screaming and crying out loud in fragility,
Because power cut disturbed the tranquillity,
Even if she's asleep she will sense that tactility.

Quite clear in her mem'ries how feeble she was before,
No confidence within herself and she just ignore,
Only a pen and paper where she can able to implore,
Knowing she can jot down what's deep within and explore,
Her silence speaks every stroke of her pen without deplore.

'Cabugao Times' and 'The Defender' was her stepping stone,
Her determination started to be grown,
Poetries and short stories must be shown,
Her leadership in Criminology nothing but a throne,

Welfare of others is literally known.

Who can tell that the frail-shy girl became an elite force?

That she managed to undergo the said Commando Course?

Two months orientation and echo-echo was the source,

Sweet-demure image totally vanished without remorse,

Automatically shifted to dour expression as she enforced.

Commando Mesmerize when will you refrain from your aspiration?

Should you totally quit your profession without confirmation?....

Or persuade the chance of your undone application...?

CHILDHOOD LIFE

High school life is nothing compared,

But now I'm telling you Primary should be shared,

Like what we're doing which was unprepared,

Yes from nowhere, look what was declared?

Cabugao North Central School our dear Alma Mater,

Where our childhood started and shapes us greater,

Naive, silliness and roguery that's now alter,

As we look back at our madness it bursts our laughter.

Facebook you're absolutely amazing,

For bringing us all together in blazing,

Who can tell that we will be rephrasing?

Adamant memoirs that lead us into star gazing.

From our wee town of Cabugao to all over the world,

Timezone may be different into which we have been hurled,

But we still manage to assimilate and furled,

And now we are living in a dream world.

Our hearts sings like a Spanish Cavalier,

Nostalgic embraces the atmosphere,

As we reminisce the past that never disappear,

Our bond was there and no one could interfere.

Now is the time to plan for others homecoming,

Setting the date for our superb upcoming,

REUNION! Yes, we were now scheming,

But as of now let's continue chatting and dreaming.

The Irony of Life

If you are famous

people will worship you,

If you have a job

people will befriend you,

If you are wealthy

people will admire you,

But once you lose them all people... will ignore you.

If you are below average student

people will mock you,

If you are poor

people will ostracise you,

If you wear inexpensive wardrobe

People will ridicule you,

But once you become fortunate... people will be your ally.

How fake the world can be?

Social media become a cup of tea,

Full of pretentious as you can see,

Be kind, don't judge and be free!

I STAND WITH THE IRON FIST

The world is in chaos,

Open fire with invisible ammo's,

Truly a deadly virus,

That attacks even the famous.

Oh, Pearl of the Orient Seas,

Commanded by the Iron Fist,

Who have had all the keys,

To shield perils that tease.

But antagonists trying to provoke,

Perplex the crisis and evoke,

Instead of helping and revoke,

United we should pray and invoke.

I may not be in our country,

But I am certainly aware.

I may not be on sentry,

But I know the nightmare.

As a Filipino I stand with you,

Beloved President that's so true,

Who has the compassion to pursue,

From the catastrophe you subdue.

Your discerning critics are daft,

Narcissistic ideology they draft,

Totally imbecile as they graft,

Shallow minded, that's all their craft.

They are few...we are many,

They can't buy us from their penny,

President Duterte we always pray,

To give you strength day by day.

We can see through your eyes,

Pain and sorrow that ties,

Undisciplined Filipinos that arise,

From your exceptional advice.

Only God is perfect,

Let your military take effect,

To finally serve and protect,

Violators...time to recollect!

APO LAKAY

(The Great President Marcos)

Heroic Ilocano and pragmatic man,
Brilliant and zealous with his plan,
Leader who is a combatant as he can,
Fight for his countrymen and not to run.

His vision for his men is crystal clear,
Welfare for every citizen and not a fear,
Eloquent speaker and candidly we cheer,
So as the world uploaded him so dear.

20 years of serving our country,
You never let even a kid hungry,
Nor brew the crowd to gets angry,
You are but Filipinos good gantry.

Your brilliance catered your wealth,
Wealth that leads their mental health,
Jealousy unveiled their dark stealth,
Awfully hated you until their last breath.

Propaganda indoctrinated many people,
Destroy your image and set unto their steeple,

You stepped down though they're feeble,
That opposition is a shameful treacle.

Philippines collapsed in just a glimpse,
Like a nightmare that comes in a blinks,
Oligarchs brought nothing but a jinx,
30 years of domination like a sphinx.

But now here comes your beloved son,
Filipinos shouting BBM! He's the one,
Your unfinished bequest must be done,
Orient Pearl's recovery no it's not a pun.

Iron Fist of Davao humbly open the gate,
For us to be once again remarkably great,
They can't no more brainwash the state,
Indeed haters gonna hate!

Tiger of the North BBM

Here comes the tiger of the north,
Roaring with victory back and forth,
Avalanche of supporters on this earth,
Waiting patiently we know the worth,
Today is the D-day of your birth.

Your victory hustle goosebumps on us,
Majority of Filipinos were making a fuss,
Uniting the people is your dealing truss,
Despite of their vague accusations,
You aim for love as your declarations.

BBM! we genially shout for triumph,
Supporters bouncing in high jump,
Behold Pearl of the Orient Sea,
Our nation will be bursting with glee,
As our new leader will lift us thee.

Filipinos let us not divide yet unite,
Colours isn't you think is right,
Coalesce and see the light,
Raise our flag and not to fight,
Stand still and be a knight.

Fellow Filipinos, truly you can never subjugate a good soul.

We Are Filipino

There is no versus between Police and Army,

Both are public servants don't make it thorny,

They are friendly forces don't cause stormy,

To serve and protect, that's their journey.

It's not about right or wrong to manifest,

Both sworn duties are not for a contest,

Either way, no rivalry should grip and detest,

Do your task without proving the best.

You are both heroes and soldier of God,

Knowledgeable in laws so it's not an odd,

To utilise any legislation, never just nod,

Comply before you complain and not to plod.

Egos and pride are sometimes the enemy,

Brotherhood however is sacred and an entity,

Yet tolerance is submissive on its clemency,

Unprejudiced is far better than enmity.

Broaden our minds is clearly a requisite,

Extinguished the tensions with etiquette,

We're battling pandemic see the evident,

We are all Filipino, but not delegates!

EGALITARIANISM

Human race might not be the same,
Black, brown, white or any name,
Tall, medium, tiny do not shame,
Your colour doesn't bring you fame.

I see myself in foreign land,
Trying to establish as I stand,
Grapple a job and manned,
But doomed drafted my hand.

I grab a pen to flare my insight,
Outlander has also a right,
Skin colour and even the height,
Doesn't define skills upright.

Barbaric ways I thought it's gone,
Inequity sadly drilling and done,
Withstanding their irrational fun,
Like a slavery that yet undone.

Visualise yin and yang together,
Equally bear cosmic energy ever,
Beyond anything and any better,

We are all human and clever.

LIFE MUST GO ON

Life is full of surprises,

As problems usually arises,
Like different franchises,
That even gives prizes.

It doesn't always sunny,
Nor jokes always funny,
But be like a super bunny,
Highly intelligent and a honey.

It might be pouring today,
But it will be fade away,
And see rainbow display,
That gives hope and an allay.

God knows every little thing,
Do good and He will bring,
Answered prayers, you ding!
Be faithful, He is the King.

So now I say life must go on,
Learn the rhythm not a con,
Enjoy the time before it's done,
Live with joy and move on.

THE LAW OF CONSIDERATION

Life is full of frustration,

People has different narration,
Behaviours that full of condemnation,
That literally turned into vexation.

Nobody's perfect in this nation,
But in God's Creation,
We should build a foundation,
And extinguished bad temptation.

Do not listen to any dictation,
However, marked like a caution,
Weigh every single allegation,
That may transpire into altercation,
Be wise and put a consolation,
Anything should need a suggestion,
'Think outside the box' is a quotation,
To ideas, scheme or plan of action,
To maintain an unending affection,
So, everything should be taken into consideration!

TO THE GALLANT SAF 44

Special Action Force, "By Skills and Virtue, We Triumph"

Hail to you heroes who fought until your last breath!

No fear to face the awaiting door of death,

To defend and secure our Motherland and the youth.

At the hour of battle field you gave your best,

You tactically crawled to range the said target,

Mike 1, Bingo! You eliminate the terrorist,

You save the innocent and the whole state.

At the time of extraction, treacherous rebels pop-out,

From nowhere they came to destroy you mercilessly,

Quite heartbreaking that reinforcement you shout!

But nobody came while you were expecting them desperately.

We are not callous how you feel that very tragic moment,

When all of you are running out of bullets...

When each of you wants to hear the voices of your loved ones...

When you brave troopers stand still and fight until your last ammos...

You are but the true heroes and will never be forgotten,

The warriors of elite force that every Filipino has proven.

Betrayal is such a torment, but SAF Family will tactfully proceed,

Because , you fallen 44 heroes deserved JUSTICE at the end.

A special breed of men like you will never just die nor fade away,

But like the "**TAGALIGTAS**" logo you will be a mainstay,

Of Philippine history as your heroism needs to display...

Salute to all of you fallen 44 SAF heroes and to all full blooded SAF!

MAY THE FORCE BE WITH YOU!!!

AWWWOOOOOOOOOAAAHHH!!!

Justice to SAF Fallen 44 Heroes and Survivors

It's been a year since that dreadful
and unimaginable episode occurred,

44 is indeed unacceptable in line of elite force
where they called the mission planning assured,
It is not only a couple of weeks or months
but years to scrutinise the said mission that was ordered,
Specialised SAF Troopers were compromised to that "OPLAN
Exodus"
just to make our Nation secure.

But leaving behind our Troopers for ten hours
is quite too long to wait for reinforcement,
Betrayal is such a morbid word
as they comply with that perilous assignment,
INJUSTICE is nevertheless but irrational,
unbearable and not even a requirement,
To Specialized Troopers who accomplished their mission
and we know it's an achievement.

JUSTICE we cried out to our fellow Troopers
who sacrificed their own lives for the sake of our nation!
We will never stand down to seek JUSTICE until the end
and truth shall prevail to that agitation,
Because you SAF Fallen 44 Heroes and Survivors
relevantly deserved JUSTICE and commendation,
Not only to the whole world but
to the orphaned children who left innocently with a question....

J-U-S-T-I-C-E

Two years to be exact when a sudden clashed
transpired,

As a SAF Trooper, to comply order is required,

Sworn duties and responsibilities never be untired,
No single murmur but a Trooper that led to be inspired.

We lost 44 brothers whose desire is placid and invincible Motherland,
Yet carnage history of SAF blasted in our native land,
Filipinos mourn deeply profound 'coz we understand,
Slaughtering heroes is not acceptable and we will stand.
Will JUSTICE prevail or will it be buried tortuously
Like our Gallant SAF 44???

IKATLONG TAON NG SAF 44

Sa Ikatlong taon ng inyong pagkalagas,
Animo'y kahapon lamang ang siyang lumipas,

'Di malilimutang bangungot ng mga Tagaligtas,

Kami'y walang sawang nagsusumamo sa nasa itaas,

Hustisya sa karumaldumal na sinapit ng ating mga Tagapagligtas.

Sa paggunita ng inyong kabayanihan aming ipagluksa,

Lungkot at hinagpis 'di makakubli, mga luha'y umaagos ng kusa,

Ngiti ng mga mahal nyo sa buhay tila naparalisa,

Tuwina'y alaala ang kahapong laging nagpapabalisa,

Pagkitil ng buhay nyo kaya nga bang maipagkakaila?

Sa bawat kilos ng inyong paggapang ng madaling araw na iyon...

Bawat hakbang niyo'ng isinagawa sa mga sandaling iyon...

Bawat pagtalsik ng pawis at dugo na para bang isang balon....

At sa bawat sigaw ng lahat na tila ba isang leon...

Tagumpay ay nakamtam sa pagpuksa ng mapanganib na si Marwan.

Mga taktikang inyong isinagawa sa pagtugis ng terorista,

Ay siyang walang sawa naming pagsuporta,

Hangga't may lupang tinatahak ipaglalaban ang hustisya,

At sa panahon ngayon kami'y nabigyan ng pag-asa,

Sapagkat ang pinakahihintay na pagbabago ay amin ng tinatamasa.

Hustisya para sa aming mga kapatid na namayapa at nakaligtas na

Tagapagligtas!

LEST WE FORGET...

Fourth year of bemoaning fellow Filipinos,
Justice wasn't served yet to our Commandos,
Whose desire is safe haven to live, I suppose,

But nightmare of SAF Troopers were impose,
Which will certainly be like hunting shadows.

01/25/2015, when our Mother Unit flooded with lamentation,
Either way, corruption was everybody's quotation,
Destroying soldiers of God is a big damnation,
That will totally devastate the hearts of the nation,
HIS chosen armies are the backbone and our foundation.

SAF 44, your heroism will never be forgotten,
Lies, greediness, and power will soon be rotten,
Grieving families let your hearts be soften,
Eventually, God will call for justice to our fallen,
Do not lose hope, nor let your faith be shortened.

BROTHERS IN ARMS....LEST WE FORGET....

SAF 44 Tragedy

Five years of wailing,
Sanction still failing,
Case might be detailing,

Justice is still utterly railing.

Legislation, why so deceptive?
Crystallise the case and be perceptive,
Human rights, why like a contraceptive?
Our brothers are human, be acceptive.

Losing 44 SAF isn't a parody,
Their lives was in jeopardy,
When there's no more remedy,
To reinforce and give energy.

Blood on hands, red in colour,
Medal is dull with hollowed valour,
Politics designed as if a glamour,
Justice! Still everybody's clamour!

Tribute To SAF 44

Gone too soon but forever be remembered,
Your loss will endlessly be treasured,
There are satirist to what you've rendered,

Whilst with dignity you have sheltered,
Protect the country like God's shepherd.

Brothers in arm the agony is still profound,
As we look at your memorial ground,
Torment is flooding and we're drowned,
The beret changes like a halo crowned.

6th years now yet it feels like yesterday,
The affliction will never just go away,
As dagger nudge deeper day-by-day,
Since you troopers met the judgement day.

Right now, we know that you're with us,
From heaven you came without a fuss,
You just came to kiss them in the puss,
Your weeping families equip them truss,
Fill their emptiness with your hearty buss.

SAF 44 7th Year Death Anniversary

Filipinos won't stop blubbering of your loss,
Perhaps for some they don't give a toss,
That your battle is quite aberrant and dross,

Yet verity dominates and grows like a moss.

Your demise is literally torturous,
Truly horrific and utterly outrageous,
Writing a poem for you is't laborious,
Your allegiance to our land is virtuous.

At this time of year SAF Troopers drop sword,
To render tribute and beseech unto the Lord,
So as to abate the grief that tied up like a cord,
Thus woeful families cluster them joy to hoard.

Time heals like they said and I can see,
As your next of kin gladly showing glee,
Our President sustain his word to free,
From a let-down ruler and a taunting tea.

This history shouldn't be repeated again,
Soldiers must tend to support not drain,
Every bullet they fire is an aid of pain,
Unshackle fear and enormity of the chain.

8 YEARS NOW...

8 years now since SAF 44 self-sacrificing,

Yet the retrospection of the past still agonising,

Melancholic memoirs nevertheless galvanising,

Our sympathies of raging need tranquilising.

Villains may perish but woe was beyond description,

Others may delineate as a design of depiction,

However, 44 doomed specialised troopers infliction,

Was a de facto of obnoxious affliction...

Every stroke of my pen writing you this poetry,

Is unparalleled to your heroism unto your country,

Shame to those derisive people for they are deviltry,

Your medal of valour is marked on the DNA of your ancestry.

Sa Kapwa ko Estudyante

Inyong panghinawakan ang isang kaganapan,

Kung saan kayo'y nakatayong busilak,

Hayaang ipakita ang nakatagong kaalaman,

Nang sa gayu'y maramdaman ang isang galak,

Ganap na maipagmamalaki kanino man!

Mga kapwa ko estudyante tayo ang pag-asa ng bayan,
Nawa'y maging inspirasyon sa susunod na kabataan,
Sa ating mga palad nakasalalay ang kinabukasan,
Inyo nang ibuga makapangyarihan nyong kakayahan,
Para sa iyong sarili, pamilya at lipunan.

Pagmasdan ang isang miserableng buhay,
Tuwina'y laging karimlan ang tinatahak,
Madalas pag walang pinag-aralan walang kaagapay,
Tila isang tuyot o lantang bulaklak,
Walang magkagusto sa dulot nitong alay.

Pagmasdan ang isang sayaw,
Walang saliw ng musika man lang,
O, konting himig para sa mananayaw,
Nang sa gayu'y magiliw ang bawat galaw,
At ganap na makamtan tunay na hirang.

Oh, pagmasdan ang taong lansangan,
Direksyon ng buhay nila'y 'di malaman,
Mga sarili'y sadyang napabayaan,
Kapit patalim kanilang hanapbuhay,
Sa mundong walang katapusang paglalakbay.
Gising na, o aking mga kapatid!
May oras pa at huwag magpadala,

Pag-aaral huwag ipagwalang bahala,
Balang araw makakamit mo din ang gantimpala,
Sa dulot nitong karangalan na walang patid!

SAAN AKO NAGKAMALI

Minahal kita ng higit sa buhay ko,
Tinanggap kita ng buong puso,
Iningatan kita ng higit sa pagkakaalam mo,
'Di ko ipinagkait ang puso kong sarado.

Pagkakaalam ko ika'y mapagkakatiwalaan,
Isang iniibig na kailangang sambahin,
Nagtiwala sa'yong di mo ko iiwan,
Ngunit lahat pala'y pawang kasinungalingan.

Saan ako nagkamali?
Bakit ika'y biglang nagbago?
Puso ko ngayo'y nagdurugo
Mundo ko'y biglang huminto.

Heto ako ngayon, tanging sarili ang yapos,
Nananalangin ng buong wagas,
Upang muling madama ang iyong haplos,
At magbalik muli sa aking landas.

TATAY DIGONG

O, kay palad naming mga Pilipino,
Sa napili naming amang pinuno,
Kamao'y bakal at dalisay ang puso,

Wasak na Inang Bayan muling nabuo,
Kami'y saludo mula't sapul na ika'y naupo.

Batikusin ka ma'y 'di kailanman magpapaantig,
Patuloy mong ipinagtatanggol aming daigdig,
'Di nagpapatinag sa anumang uri ng pagliligalig,
Maisalba lamang ang bansang puno ng adik,
At naglipanang kawatan at mga pinunong may baltik.

Tatay Digong kayo ang sugo ng Panginoon,
Sapagkat ang lubog na bansa'y dapat ng mai-ahon,
Mula sa karalitaan at kamay ng mga mandarambong,
O, Agila ng Davao walang takot mong sinalubong,
Mga nakaatang at nagbabadyang panganib mula sa mga damuhong.

Aanhin mo ang tila Santo sa'ting mga mata,
Kung ang mithii'y maghasik ng di kanais-nais sa lupa,
Mabuti pa si Tatay Digong kahit siya'y nagmumura,
Puso'y walang kasing busilak para sa madla,
May paninindigan sa kanyang panunumpa.

Ipinagmamalaki ka namin sa sanlibutan,
Sapagkat muling umugong ating Inang Bayan,
Sa buong mundo kayo'y tunay na hinahangaan,
Mga banyaga'y kayo ang nais sa kanilang pamahalaan,

At kami'y nagagalak sa iyong kadakilaan.

Taos puso ang aming pasasalamat,
Sa kasaysayan ika'y walang dudang isusulat,
Tunay kang bayani at aming isisiwalat,
Hanggang sa dulo laban mo'y laban ng lahat,
Tatay Digong salamat kami'y iyong minulat!

INANG KALIKASAN

Pagmasdan ang ating kapaligiran,
Kay gandang mga puno't halaman,
Kulay nila'y sadya ngang luntian,
Na nagbibigay lamig sa'ting tahanan.

Pagmasdan mo ang ating karagatan,
Munting alon nila'y tila kinakantahan,
Ng malamig simoy hanging amihan,
Asul nyang kulay ay gaya ng kalangitan.

O, pagmasdan ang ating kabundukan,
Bantayog nito'y iyong masisilayan,
Mula sa maaliwas na kapatagan,
Kagandaha'y hindi pagsasawahan.

Ngunit tila karikita'y nabalewala,
Ng mga gahaman at walang kwenta,
Niluray ng husto at kanilang sinira,
Likas na kagandahan biglang naluha.

Sa isang iglap dumating ang kalamidad,
Matinding baha umabot sa siyudad,
Mga basurang tinapo'y bumaliktad,
Bumalik sa'tin ang unos at isinagad.

Palahaw nati'y sadyang nakakarindi,
Mahal natin sa buhay biglang nasawi,

Kayamanan nati'y biglang binawi,
At ngayon nga'y paano ka babawi?

Inang kalikasan ika'y makapangyarihan,
Sa taong 2020 ikaw nga ba'y nasiyahan?
Pagkat ika'y nakapagpahingang tuluyan,
Mula sa kamay ng malulupit na tauhan.

Magsilbi nawang panimula ngayong taon,
Kapaligira'y ingatan ng habang panahon,
Pagyamanin lahat at huwag nating ibaon,
Ang aral ng kalikasa'y tutubong tila dahon.

Maligayang Araw Ng Mga Nanay

Sa araw na ito kami'y pumupugay ,
Sapagkat isa kang dakilang tunay,
Na walang sawang gumagabay,

Sa'ming magkakapatid Nanay.

Ilaw ka ng ating munting tahanan,
Walang kapaguran kahit kailan,
Gagawin lahat para matutunan,
Buhay sa mundong ginagalawan.

Nanay ipinagmamalaki ka namin,
Sa buong buhay ikaw aming salamin,
Lahat ng pagkakamali'y tutuwirin,
Ano mang unos iyong tatawirin.

Sakripisyo mo'y di mapapantayan,
Sa pagpapalaki sa aming tuluyan,
Pag-aaruga sami'y iyong kasiyahan,
Kahit ikaw Nanay ay nahihirapan.

Sa lahat ng 'Super Mum' sa mundo,
Kami'y tunay ngang sumasaludo,
Sa inyong dalisay na pagkatao,
Karapat-dapat kayong ikwento.

Nanay para sa iyo ang aking tula,

Mensahe ko'y hindi nakakalula,

Sapagkat tunay kang dakila,

Mahal ka namin saksi mga tala.

Dakila Ka Ina

Puso mo'y sadyang dalisay,

Pag-aaruga'y napakahusay,

Gagawin lahat iyan ni Nanay,

Sa pamilya dakila kang tunay.

Martir ka man sa pagmamahal,
Noo'y tila isang takot at hangal,
Pamilyang buo iyon ang banal,
Kahit nahihirapan sarili'y isusugal.

Ngunit ngayo'y buo ang katapangan,
Haharapin anumang kaganapan,
Kinabukasan ng anak at kapakanan,
Lumbay ay titikisin sa kaisipan.

Ikaw ang tanglaw sa dilim, oh, Ina,
Taglay mong katangian ay kakaiba,
Hindi kailanman matitinag sa kaba,
Layunin mo'y mga anak na maisalba.

Maligayang Araw ng mga Tatay

Haligi ka ng aming tahanan Itay,
Kung kayat ito'y sadyang matibay,
Ikaw ang nagsisilbing kaagapay,

Ano mang unos ang *sumalakay*.

Gagawin mo lahat para sa'ting pamilya,
Titiisin anumang trabaho ito'y kinakaya,
Sakripisyo mo ay hindi maipagkakaila,
Magisnan lamang ang saya sa mga mata.

Mga anak mo'ng *naghihintay* sa'yong pag-uwi,
Pagod at hirap mo ay biglang napapawi,
Sapagkat mga inosenteng *ngiti* ay nakakawili,
Na sa isang iglap *dinaramdam* mo ay naikukubli.

Tatay, hindi ka man kasing bihasa ni Inay,
Sa pag-alaga samin sa araw-araw sa bahay,
Ngunit alam ng Diyos dakila kang tunay,
Ibibigay lahat ng lakas para kami'y mabuhay.

Sa araw na ito binabati ka namin aming Ama,
Isang *pagpupugay* sa lahat ng mga Papa,
Ipinagmamalaki namin kayo Tatang, Dad, Dada,
Saludo kami sa walang sawa nyong pagpapahalaga!

PANDEMYA

Ikaw pandemya biglang dumating,
Sa buhay naming puno ng ningning,
Ni walang abiso ng ika'y kumiling,

Sa mundong kailanma'y 'di ka hiniling.

Sa unang salta mo sa bansang Tsina,
Animo'y pangkaraniwang sakit tuwina,
Datapwa't kami'y nagkamali sa kanila,
Nang mapanood namin ang mga balita.

Pandemya kinitil mo ang milyong buhay,
Ikaw ay sadyang nakakahawang tunay,
Mga eksperto sabi'y hindi ka masaway,
Sa dulot mong panganib na pasaway.

Buong lupalop inihasik mo ang delubyo,
Ekonomiya'y ginawa mong kalbaryo,
Mga tao'y nawalan ng matinong trabaho,
Pagkat ika'y nasa labas at naglalaro.

Araw-araw pagkabalisa iyong idinulot,
Sa kaibuturan nami'y iyong tinuyot,
Depresyon ng iba'y iyo ring binalot,
Dahil sa kanilang balitang katakot-takot.

Ngunit unti-unti'y aking napagtanto,

Hindi kaya ika'y matagal ng planado?

Ng mga makapangyarihan sa mundo?

Wag tayong palinlang at isipa'y isarado.

Manalig nawa tayo sa Poong Maykapal,

Sapagkat Sya lang ang tunay na banal,

Sa mundo nating puno ng karumaldumal,

Maging mapagmasid at Diyos nyang kawal.

Printed in Poland
by Amazon Fulfillment
Poland Sp. z o.o., Wrocław
18 July 2023